THROUGH THE SEASONS

Wood

Deni Bown

Illustrated by Wendy Meadway

Through the Seasons

Field and Hedgerow
Garden
Park
Pond
Stream
Wood

Edited by Philippa Smith
Designed by Charles Harford HSD

First published in 1989 by
Wayland (Publishers) Ltd
61 Western Road, Hove
East Sussex BN3 1JD, England

British Library Cataloguing in Publication Data
Bown, Deni
Wood. — (Through the seasons).
1. Great Britain. Organisms. Habitats
I. Title II. Meadway, Wendy III. Series
574.5'2

ISBN 1 85210 754 5

Phototypeset by D.P. Press, Sevenoaks, Kent
Printed in Italy by G. Canale & C.S.p.A., Turin
Bound in Belgium by Casterman S.A.

CONTENTS

Words that appear in **bold** in the text
are explained in the glossary on page 30.

WHAT IS A WOOD?

A wood is where many trees grow together.

Large woods are called forests. There are woods and forests in most countries of the world. They are a very important part of the countryside. We enjoy seeing woods and exploring them. We depend on woods for **timber** and other products, such as materials for making paints and medicines. The roots of the trees hold the soil together and prevent **erosion**, especially on steep hillsides. When trees are **felled**, the soil is washed away by the rain.

Many trees lose their leaves in winter so that they are not damaged by frost and snow. Trees that do this are called **deciduous**. Oak, ash, beech, horse chestnut and larch are deciduous. **Evergreen** trees keep their leaves all year round. Yew, holly and pine are evergreens.

In woods it is damp and shady, even on sunny days.

The tallest trees form a **canopy** of leaves above the ground, rather like an umbrella or sunshade. Below them is an **understorey** of smaller trees and bushes. The tree canopy protects the plants and animals beneath from heavy rain, hot sun and strong winds.

Most woods have many different kinds of trees. You can tell each kind by the shape of its leaves.

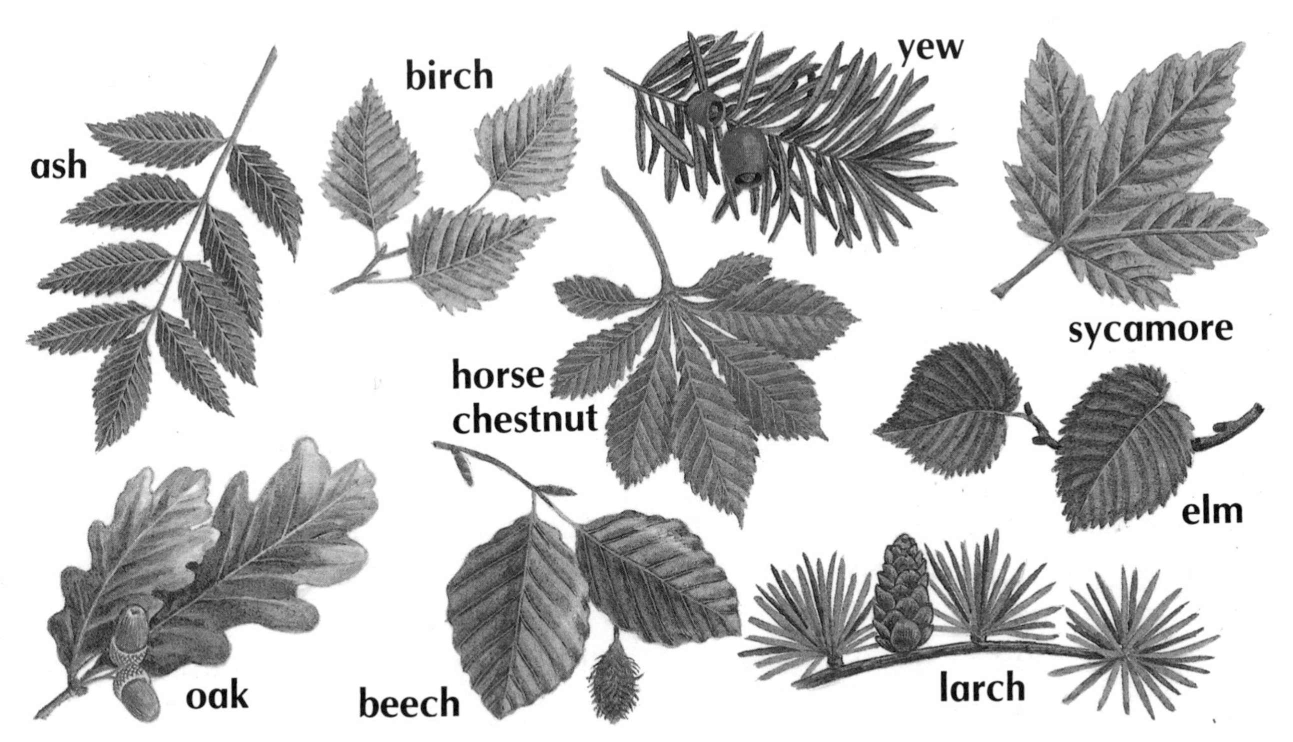

Horse chestnut buds are known as stickybuds.
In spring, the sticky covering splits and the leaves open.

The trees show signs of growth quite early in spring, as the days start to get longer and warmer. Each new leaf is tightly folded inside a bud. The buds swell as the tiny leaves grow. Eventually they split open and the delicate leaves unfold. At first they are a fresh bright green and have a soft, sometimes downy texture.

Oak trees flower in spring. ▶

Both male and female flowers are needed for a tree to produce seeds. Some trees have large, colourful flowers but many have small, greenish ones that you can hardly see. Oak tree flowers are easy to miss. The male flowers hang in clusters called catkins. They produce **pollen**. The female flowers are small and round. They start to grow into acorns as soon as the pollen touches them.

◀ The female cones of the larch tree are pink and soft.

The larch tree bears cones instead of flowers. Male and female cones are quite different. The pink female cone is known as a larch rose, because it looks rather like a flower. The male cone (lower down the twig) is still in bud and not ready to produce pollen. The young larch twig has tufts of new leaves.

Tiny young beech trees begin to grow from beech nuts.

Although seeds fall to the ground in autumn, they remain **dormant** until the spring. They must be warm, damp and in darkness before they can **germinate**. Then they need light to grow into young **seedlings**. The first leaves that grow from a seed are called the seed leaves. They are a different shape from the true leaves. Two of the seedlings in the picture have just got their first pair of true leaves. Not all beech nuts germinate. Some land on top of dead leaves and become dry and shrivelled.

Bluebells grow new leaves and flower in spring.

The bluebell plant grows from a **bulb** which looks a bit like an onion. The bulb stores food and water so that the plant can stay alive when the ground is too dry or too cold, or when there is not enough light for it to grow. In late summer and autumn, bluebell plants are dormant and have no roots or leaves, only bulbs. By late spring, the leaves have grown and the plants flower, filling the air with a lovely scent which attracts bees.

Ramsons like bare wet soil in woods.

Like bluebells, ramsons grow from bulbs and flower in spring. The two kinds of plants are usually found in different parts of the wood because ramsons prefer wetter soil. Ramsons have clusters of star-shaped flowers. The whole plant smells strongly of garlic.

Birds build their nests in spring.

This bird is called a mistle thrush because it likes to eat mistletoe berries. The parent birds build their nest from grass, twigs, soil and moss which they collect here and there in the wood. The female usually lays four eggs. About two weeks later the eggs hatch. Baby birds grow quickly and need a lot of food. The parent birds are busy hunting for insects and worms all day long.

Baby fallow deer are born in the spring. They are called fawns.

Many animals give birth in the spring because there is plenty of food for them and their young. A fawn can walk and eat grass as soon as it is born, although it also needs milk from its mother. The fawn's spotted coat is a good disguise in the dappled light of the woodland.

THINGS TO DO IN SPRING

When you go for a walk in the woods, look under the biggest trees for seedlings. Some trees take fifty years before they are large enough to produce seeds. Seedlings are eaten by deer, rabbits and insect pests, so few ever become **mature** trees. If you find any acorns or beech nuts that are not yet growing, take one home to plant in a pot of soil. It will soon sprout a shoot and a root if it is kept warm and damp.

After a few years, a seedling has a strong, slender woody stem and is called a **sapling**. Can you see any saplings? If an old tree is blown down by the wind, the saplings around it grow quickly because there is more light.

Look for some woodland flowers. Perhaps you already know their names. If not, ask someone to show you a book about wild flowers and see if you can find out what they are called.

New fern leaves are curled up like a fist. This makes them stronger.

Try to find a fern plant and look at the shape of the new leaves. They are sometimes called crooks because their shape is like a shepherd's crook.

When you get home, think of all the leaves and flowers you have seen and draw a picture of them together in a bunch.

Leaves on a tree spread out so that each catches the sun.

Plants feed in a different way from animals. They use their roots to absorb water and dissolved plant foods from the soil, but they can also make some of their own food from water, air and sunlight. This is done by the leaves. Each leaf is like a factory. It contains thousands of tiny green **cells** which turn water and air into food, using the sun's energy. To work properly, every leaf must be held so that it catches the sun. You can see how carefully the beech leaves in the picture are arranged. This pattern is called the **leaf mosaic**.

◀ Ferns can grow in very shady places.

By summer, all the leaves on the trees are fully grown and have turned dark green. Only a few shafts of light pass through the canopy and understorey to the woodland floor. Some plants, such as ferns and ivy, can grow in low levels of light.

Foxgloves often grow in areas where trees have been cut down. ▶

Foxglove plants grow from seeds that are as small as grains of sand. In the first year, they only have leaves. The next summer, they flower. After flowering they die, leaving thousands of seeds to take their place. When an area of trees in the wood is felled, the ground beneath suddenly receives much more light. Foxglove plants in the clearing can then begin to grow. The following summer, they all flower together.

◀ **The spots on these oak leaves are silk button galls.**

The insects that made these **galls** are very small black wasps. They lay their eggs in the oak leaf. When the **larvae** hatch out, they irritate the leaf, rather like a splinter inside your finger. To stop the irritation, the cells around the larvae grow into a gall to seal off the damage from the rest of the leaf.

There are many different kinds of galls.

Wood ants make big nests from twigs and leaves. ►

The actual nest is in a tree stump or underground, but the mound may be over a metre high. As many as a million ants live in a **colony**. They all work together to look after the nest. Wood ants are fierce insects. They will attack and eat almost any very small animal, including insects and other ants.

◄ **A young tawny owl. Owls hunt at night for mice and other animals.**

Although tawny owls are common in woodland, they are rarely seen because they sleep during the day. They usually roost on a branch, close to the tree trunk. Smaller birds are frightened of owls, and if they find one roosting, they squawk noisily to scare it away. Tawny owls never build nests. They lay their eggs in the old nests of squirrels or in a hole in a tree.

The badger comes out at night to search for food.

Badgers live deep underground in a large hole called a set. Badgers are not fast or fierce hunters, so they eat whatever they can find. Mostly they eat insects, slugs, worms, roots, leaves and fruits, but sometimes they may eat weak or injured animals, such as baby birds that have fallen out of the nest.

Badgers have short legs but their bodies are up to a metre long. Newborn badger cubs have silver-grey fur. By the time they are old enough to leave the set, they are dark grey with black-and-white striped faces. This colouring is a good **camouflage** against the shadows of a moonlit wood.

See if you can find some foxglove plants in a wood. You may be able to find plants of all ages. (Do not handle foxgloves, as they are poisonous.) Young plants have only leaves. When they are fully grown, they have larger leaves and spikes of flowers. The flowers open one by one up the stem and are visited by bumble bees looking for **nectar**.

Foxglove plants do not flower in their first year.

After flowering, the seed pods develop. The plants slowly die when the seeds have ripened and dropped from the pods, but the dead plants take a long time to decay. Make several drawings to show the **life cycle** of a foxglove.

You may not be lucky enough to see a tawny owl, but you may discover where it roosts. Owls cannot **digest** some parts of their prey, such as fur, bones and insects' wings, so they bring them up as pellets. If you find these remains under a tree, you can be sure that the owl roosts there.

Oak trees and wild rose bushes are good places to find galls. Each kind of gall is made by a different wasp. Gall wasps are hard to spot, but there is no danger in looking for them as they do not sting. Look carefully among the leaves of trees, saplings and other plants in the wood. How many different galls can you find?

AUTUMN

In autumn most trees change colour and lose their leaves.

Autumn is a time of great change in woods and forests. Deciduous trees prepare for winter by dropping their leaves. In North America autumn is called the fall. Trees lose water through their leaves, just as we perspire through our skin. Like us, they get thirsty! The tree must replace the lost water by taking in more from the soil through its roots. In winter, it cannot always do this because the water in the ground is often frozen. Dropping its leaves stops the tree from losing too much water at a time when it may not be able to make up for the loss.

The leaves slowly turn from green to yellow and brown.

Before a tree loses its leaves, the food in them goes back into the twigs. This is what makes them change colour. When all the food has left the leaves, they fall off, leaving a scar where the stalk was joined to the twig.

Fruits such as beech nuts ripen in autumn and fall to the ground.

The fruits of woodland trees are sometimes called **mast**. A beech tree produces thousands of nuts each year. They develop inside prickly green husks which are lined with soft silky hairs. When ripe, they turn brown and split into four-pointed stars to release the nuts.

◀ Woodlice feed on fallen leaves.

The woodlouse is not an insect, but a relative of shrimps and crabs. It has seven pairs of legs and a pair of feelers which help it to find its way around. Its body is divided into segments. When alarmed, it rolls into a ball. Woodlice live in damp places under logs and stones.

Many fungi are poisonous. ▶

The best time to find fungi is in the autumn. Fungi are parts of strange underground plants. They do not have leaves and flowers like most plants. The part hidden underground looks like a cobweb of threads. The threads grow through dead leaves or wood, taking in food from them and helping to rot them down. The part you see is rather like a fruit. It produces **spores** which will grow into new fungi. The spores are as fine as dust.

Nuts are the favourite food of nuthatches.

Nuthatches look for acorns, hazel nuts and beech mast in the woods. When they find a nut, they wedge it into a crack in the bark of a tree. Then they break open the hard shell by hammering it with their beak. You can often tell from a distance if a bird is a nuthatch by the odd way that it runs down tree trunks head first.

Autumn is a very busy time for birds and animals. They must eat as much as possible so that they are big and healthy for the cold winter ahead. Most nuts and seeds are eaten by birds and animals, so few are left to grow.

Nothing goes to waste in woods. When the leaves fall, they rot down into soil and make food for the trees.

millipede woodlouse bristletail worm false scorpion

All the living things in a wood depend on each other. Trees make some of their own food through the leaves, but they also need special foods from the soil. When leaves and twigs fall in autumn, they form a thick layer called litter.

Different kinds of fungi begin to push their way up through the leaf litter. Fungi and small animals, such as woodlice, worms and millipedes, feed on the dead leaves, breaking them down into waste which the trees' roots can then feed on.

THINGS TO DO IN AUTUMN

The autumn is the most colourful time in the woods and on dry days the thick layer of fallen leaves is fun to walk through. Gather some of the most beautiful leaves and draw round each one on a piece of paper. Then paint them all the different autumn colours.

Look under a piece of dead wood or beneath the leaf litter. You will be surprised how many creatures may be living there. As well as woodlice, there may be slugs, worms, centipedes or beetles. If you carefully break open a chunk of rotten wood, you may see the white threads of a fungus plant. Whenever you disturb living things, you should put them back as you found them so that they are not harmed.

Fungi are fascinating but you must take great care when investigating them. Many are poisonous, even to touch, and breathing in the spores is bad for your lungs. See if you can **identify** any fungi that you find in the wood. You will need a book which shows pictures of the different kinds. Remember to look on tree trunks as well as on the ground. Although fungi may be poisonous to us, some animals can eat them. You may see the teeth marks of squirrels or holes made by slugs.

The bracket fungus lives on trees.

WINTER

The trees are often weighed down with snow in the winter.

As autumn turns to winter, mist and dew are turned to freezing fog and frost. On some mornings, everything is crisp and white, and pools of water are covered with a thick layer of ice. If it rains when the weather is very cold, the rain water is frozen too and it comes down as hail or snow. Hard frosts and thick snow make life very difficult for animals. They may have to scratch through the snow to find food and go a long way in their search for a drink of water.

The leaves of holly trees are thick and shiny.

Evergreen trees stand out clearly in winter when the other trees are bare. Their leaves have a waxy coating which stops them losing too much water. It also helps to shed snow so that the branches do not break under the weight. Evergreens make new leaves in the spring and lose their old ones a few at a time, all through the year.

Squirrels have stores of nuts for the winter.

Squirrels dig holes and bury some of the nuts they find. Although they may sleep through the very cold days of winter, they do not **hibernate**, so storing food is a good way of making sure that there will be enough to eat.

◀ **Tree trunks are often covered with mosses.**

Winter is the best time of the year for looking at some of the smallest plants of all – mosses, **lichen** and **algae**. You will need a **magnifying glass** to see them properly. They like damp places, especially the sides of trees which are shaded from the sun.

Even when the trees are bare, you can tell the different kinds by their twigs.

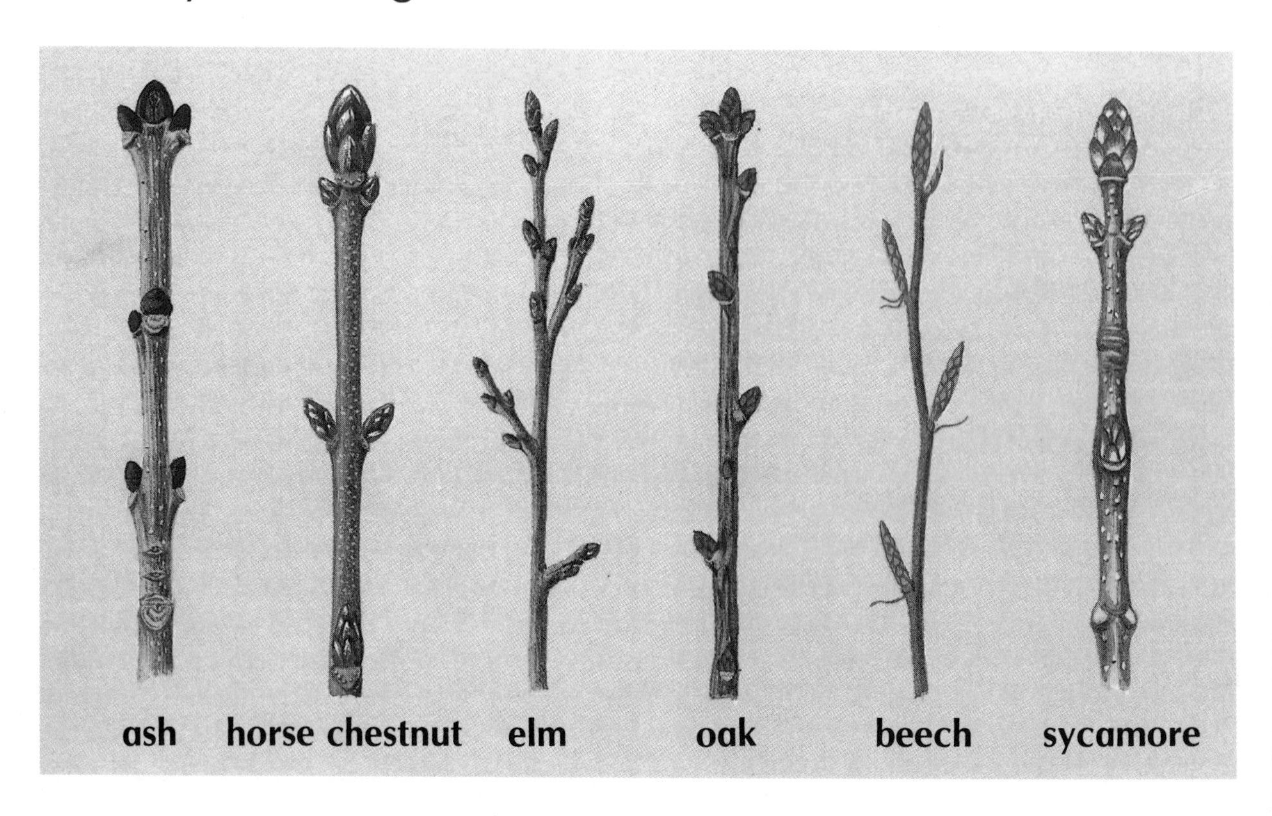

Make bark rubbings of several trees in the wood. The bark of each kind of tree has a different colour and texture. Beech trees have smooth grey bark but that of oaks is brownish-grey with deep cracks. You will need pieces of paper and wax crayons. Greaseproof paper works well and you should use the flat side of the crayon. It is easier if you attach the paper to the bark, using parcel tape, or ask a friend to hold it for you. Remember to write the name of each tree on the rubbing.

If you look very carefully among the dead leaves on the woodland floor, you may find a skeleton leaf. All the soft parts of the leaf have rotted away, leaving a lacy network of veins. You can make your own leaf skeletons. Put some large leaves in a container of water and leave until they have gone soft and slimy. It may take a month or more. Rinse them under the tap, gently removing the soft parts with your fingers or a small paintbrush. When the skeleton leaf has dried, it can be pressed between sheets of paper with several heavy books on top. The leaves can be painted to make Christmas decorations, but you will need to do it very gently, using a very soft brush and making sure that the paint is not too thick.

Skeleton leaves are very beautiful.

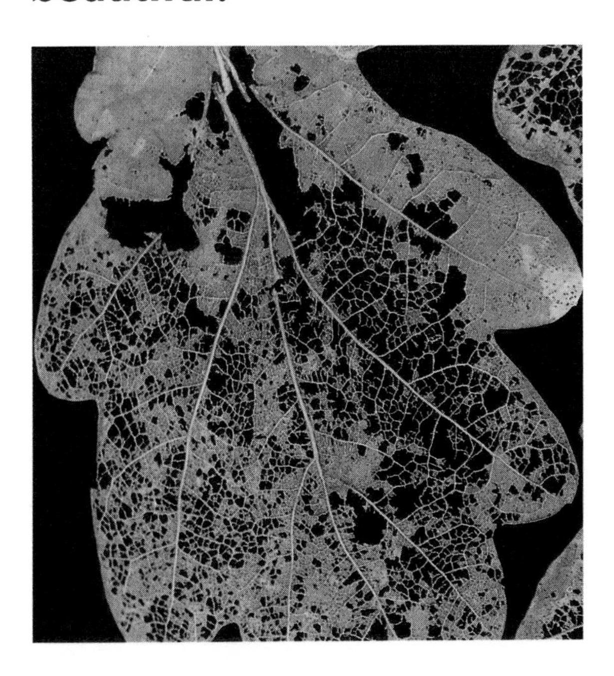

Spring
Summer

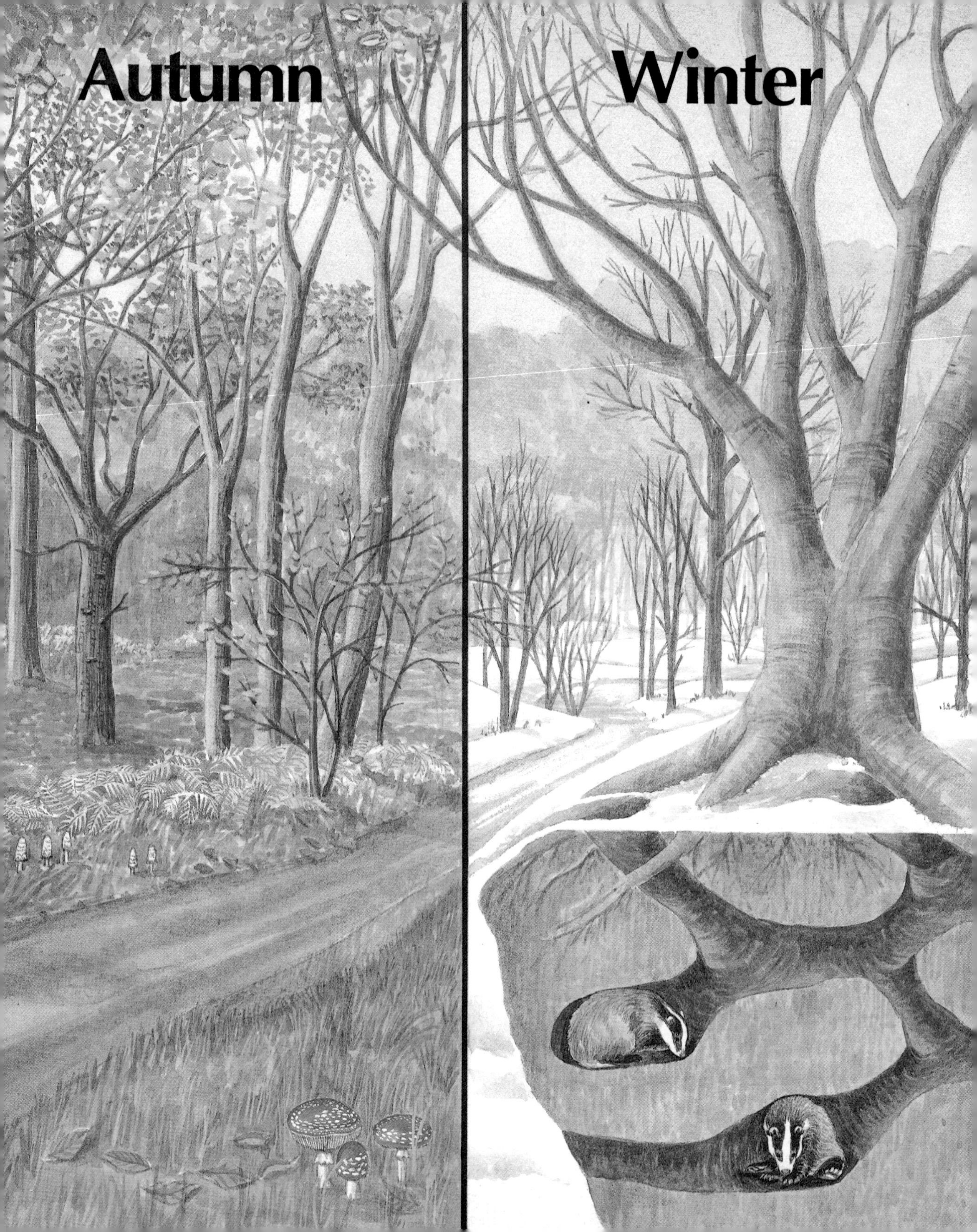
Autumn
Winter

GLOSSARY

Algae Plants that have no proper stems, roots or leaves and grow in damp places.

Bulb The underground part of certain plants, such as bluebells, in which food is stored.

Camouflage Colouring which makes an animal blend in with its surroundings so that it is not seen by enemies.

Canopy The tops of the largest trees in a wood.

Cells The smallest parts of any living thing.

Colony A group of animals of the same kind which live together (for example, ants).

Deciduous A deciduous tree is one that loses all its leaves at the end of the growing season.

Digest To dissolve food in the stomach.

Dormant Alive but not moving or growing.

Erosion The wearing away of soil by water.

Evergreen Bearing leaves all through the year.

Felled Cut down.

Gall A growth on trees (especially oaks) caused by an insect.

Germinate To begin to grow.

Hibernate To go into a sleep-like state during the winter.

Identify To find out the name of a plant or animal.

Larvae The stage that some animals go through after they have hatched from eggs but before they turn into adults (for example, the grubs of gall wasps).

Leaf mosaic The way that leaves are arranged so that each leaf gets as much light as possible.

Lichen Tiny, fungus-like plants.

Life cycle The different stages in the life of a plant or animal.

Magnifying glass A glass lens which makes small things look bigger.

Mast The fruit of woodland trees (for example, beech nuts and acorns).

Mature Fully grown.

Nectar A sugary liquid produced by flowers.

Pollen Powder produced by

male flowers which makes the female flowers develop seeds.

Sapling A young tree.

Seedlings Very young plants.

Spores The tiny round cells of certain plants (such as ferns and fungi) which will grow into new plants.

Timber Wood cut up for building purposes.

Understorey The bushes and smaller trees in a wood.

BOOKS TO READ

Conker by Barrie Watts (A. & C. Black, 1987).

Discovering Fungi by Jennifer Coldrey (Wayland, 1987).

Discovering Trees by Jill Bailey (Wayland, 1988).

Forest Calendar by Irmgard Lucht (A. & C. Black, 1987).

Grey Squirrel by Jennifer Coldrey (Deutsch, 1982).

In the Woods by Sarah McKenzie (Wayland, 1985).

The Life Cycle of a Tree by John Williams (Wayland, 1988).

The New Observer's Book of Wild Flowers by Francis Rose (Frederick Warne, 1978).

The Tree and Its World by Romola Showell (Ladybird, 1975).

Tree in a Wood by Jan Ethelberg (A. & C. Black, 1980).

The World of the Ant by H. and A. Fischer-Nagel (Dent, 1985).

Picture acknowledgements

All photographs were taken by Deni Bown with the exception of the following: Chris Fairclough Colour Library 10 (both), 15 (below), 16, 20 (top), 21, cover.

INDEX